"Maybe that's what life is... a wink of the eye and winking stars." ~ j.k.

Don't use the phone.
People are never ready to
answer it. Use poetry.

jack kerouac's
little book of
selected quotes

Sure baby, mañana. It was always mañana. For the next few weeks that was all I heard--mañana a lovely word and one that probably means heaven.

ck kerouac's
ttle book of
ected quotes

I saw that my life was
a vast glowing empty
page and I could do
anything I wanted.

jack kerouac's
little book of
selected quotes

My shoes are clean from
walking in the rain.

One man practicing
kindness in the
wilderness is worth
all the temples this
world pulls.

jack kerouac's
little book of
selected quotes

I realized either I was crazy or the world was crazy; and I picked on the world. And of course I was right.

Colleges being nothing but grooming schools for the middle-class non-identity which usually finds its perfect expression on the outskirts of the campus in rows of well-to-do houses with lawns and television sets in each living room with everybody looking at the same thing and thinking the same thing at the same time while the Japhies of the world go prowling in the wilderness to hear the voice crying in the wilderness, to find the ecstacy of the stars, to find the dark mysterious secret of the origin of faceless wonderless crapulous civilization.

The fact that everybody
in the world dreams every
night ties all mankind
together.

ck kerouac's
ttle book of
ected quotes

What's in store for me
in the direction I
don't take?

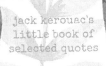

jack kerouac's
little book of
selected quotes

I felt like lying down by the side
of the trail and remembering it
all. The woods do that to you,
they always look familiar, long
lost, like the face of a long-dead
relative, like an old dream,
like a piece of forgotten song
drifting across the water, most
of all like golden eternities of
past childhood or past manhood
and all the living and the dying
and the heartbreak that went on a
million years ago and the clouds
as they pass overhead seem to
testify (by their own lonesome
familiarity) to this feeling.

ck kerouac's
ttle book of
ected quotes

Remove literary, grammatical and syntactical inhibition.

jack kerouac's
little book of
selected quotes

Better to sleep in an
uncomfortable bed free,
than sleep in a
comfortable bed unfree.

Be in love with your life,
every detail of it.

jack kerouac's
little book of
selected quotes

No man should go through
life without once
experiencing healthy,
even bored solitude in
the wilderness, finding
himself depending solely
on himself and thereby
learning his true and
hidden strength.

ck kerouac's
ttle book of
ected quotes

The only truth is music.

jack kerouac's
little book of
selected quotes

Let nature do the
freezing and frightening
and isolating in this
world. let men work and
love and fight it off.

I promise I shall never
give up, and that I'll die
yelling & laughing.

jack kerouac's
little book of
selected quotes

I was halfway across America, at the dividing line between the East of my youth and the West of my future.

Don't drink to get drunk.
Drink to enjoy life.

jack kerouac's
little book of
selected quotes

If you tell a true story,
you can't be wrong.

ck kerouac's
ttle book of
ected quotes

He had no place he could stay in without getting tired of it and because there was nowhere to go but everywhere, keep rolling under the stars.

jack kerouac's
little book of
selected quotes

If you own a rug
you own too much.

Suppose we suddenly
wake up and see that
what we thought to be
this and that, ain't
this and that at all?

jack kerouac's
little book of
selected quotes

Because in the end, you
won't remember the time
you spent working in
the office or mowing
your lawn. Climb that
goddamn mountain.

What does it mean that I am in this endless universe, thinking that I'm a man sitting under the stars on the terrace of the earth, but actually empty and awake throughout the emptiness and awakedness of everything? It means that I'm empty and awake, that I know I'm empty and awake, and that there's no difference between me and anything else.

Everything is ecstasy inside. We just don't know it because of our thinking-minds. But in our true blissful essence of mind [it] is known that everything is alright forever and forever and forever.

Roaring dreams take place in a perfectly silent mind. Now that we know this, throw the raft away.

I hope it is true that a
man can die and yet not
only live in others but
give them life, and not
only life, but that great
consciousness of life.

I promise I shall never
give up, and that I'll die
yelling and laughing,
and that until then I'll
rush around this world I
insist is holy and pull
at everyone's lapel and
make them confess to me
and to all.

I rather like the idea of having all my hours to myself: eating a Fudge Sundae, watching a movie, sleeping on my couch, singing in the bathroom, studying the woods, kidding around with a girl, playing cards lazily – all kinds of stuff that American brands 'shiftless.'

ck kerouac's
ttle book of
ected quotes

I came to a point where I
needed solitude and just
stop the machine of
'thinking' and 'enjoying'
what they call 'living',
I just wanted to lie in
the grass and look
at the clouds.

jack kerouac's
little book of
selected quotes

I like too many things
and get all confused
and hung-up running
from one falling star
to another till i drop.
This is the night, what
it does to you. I had
nothing to offer
anybody except my
own confusion.

You aren't ever going to
be anything in this
world unless you do
what you want to do,
when you want to do it--
don't plan anything,
just go out and do it.

jack kerouac's
little book of
selected quotes

Something great is
about to happen to me:
I'm about to love
somebody very much.

I realized that I had died
and been reborn numberless
times but just didn't
remember because the
transitions from life to
death and back are so
ghostly easy, a magical
action for naught, like
falling asleep and waking
up again a million times,
the utter casualness and
deep ignorance of it.

jack kerouac's
little book of
selected quotes

Desolation,
desolation, I owe so
much to desolation.

How I wished I'd have had a camera of my own, a mad mental camera that could register pictorial shots, of the photographic artist himself prowling about for his ultimate shot – an epic in itself. (On the road with Robert Frank, 1958)

Isn't it true that you start your life a sweet child believing in everything under your father's roof? Then comes the day of the Laodiceans, when you know you are wretched and miserable and poor and blind and naked, and with the visage of a gruesome grieving ghost you go shuddering through nightmare life.

No matter how you travel,
how 'successful' your
tour, or foreshortened,
you always learn
something and learn to
change your thoughts.

All of life is a
foreign country.

Boys and girls in America have such a sad time together; sophistication demands that they submit to sex immediately without proper preliminary talk. Not courting talk – real straight talk about souls, for life is holy and every moment is precious.

jack kerouac's little book of selected quotes

As we crossed the
Colorado-Utah border
I saw God in the sky in
the form of huge gold
sunburning clouds
above the desert that
seemed to point a
finger at me and say,
"Pass here and go on,
you're on the road
to heaven."

ck kerouac's
ttle book of
ected quotes

On soft Spring nights I'll
stand in the yard under
the stars – Something
good will come out of all
things yet – And it will
be golden and eternal
just like that –
There's no need to
say another word.

jack kerouac's
little book of
selected quotes

Ah, if I could realize, if
I could forget myself and
devote my meditations to
the freeing, the
awakening and the
blessedness of all living
creatures everywhere I'd
realize what there is,
is ecstasy.

Maybe that's what life is... a wink of the eye and winking stars.

jack kerouac's
little book of
selected quotes

Rest and be kind,
you don't have to
prove anything.

If critics say your work stinks it's because they want it to stink and they can make it stink by scaring you into conformity with their comfortable little standards. Standards so low that they can no longer be considered "dangerous" but set in place in their compartmental understandings.

the only people for me are
the mad ones, the ones
who are mad to live, mad
to talk, mad to be saved,
desirous of everything at
the same time, the ones
who never yawn or say a
commonplace thing, but
burn, burn, burn like
fabulous yellow roman
candles exploding like
spiders across the stars.

ck kerouac's
ttle book of
ected quotes

My aunt once said that
the world would never
find peace until men fell
at their women's feet and
asked for forgiveness.

The best teacher is
experience and not
through someone's
distorted point of view.

All I wanted to do was sneak out into the night and disappear somewhere, and go and find out what everybody was doing all over the country.

Pain or love or danger
makes you real again.

I realized these were all the snapshots which our children would look at someday with wonder, thinking their parents had lived smooth, well-ordered lives and got up in the morning to walk proudly on the sidewalks of life, never dreaming the raggedy madness and riot of our actual lives, our actual night, the hell of it, the senseless emptiness.

jack kerouac's little book of selected quotes

Thinking of the stars night
after night I begin to
realize 'The stars are words'
and all the innumerable
worlds in the Milky Way are
words, and so is this world
too. And I realize that no
matter where I am, whether
in a little room full of
thought, or in this endless
universe of stars and
mountains, it's all
in my mind.

ck kerouac's
ttle book of
ected quotes

One day I will find the
right words, and they
will be simple.

jack kerouac's
little book of
selected quotes

I want a blaze of light to flame in me forever in a timeless, dear love of everything. And why should I pretend to want anything else?

My eyes were glued on
life and they were
full of tears.

You are the equal of the
idol who has given you
your inspiration.

ck kerouac's
ttle book of
ected quotes

I was surprised, as
always, be how easy
the act of leaving
was, and how good it
felt. The world was
suddenly rich with
possibility.

jack kerouac's
little book of
selected quotes

Put down the pen someone
else gave you. No one ever
drafted a life worth
living on borrowed ink.

Who knows, my God, but that the universe is not one vast sea of compassion actually, the veritable holy honey, beneath all this show of personality and cruelty?

jack kerouac's
little book of
selected quotes

The road must eventually
lead to the whole world.

ck kerouac's
ttle book of
ected quotes

You'd be surprised
how little I knew
even up to yesterday.

Live, travel, adventure,
bless, and don't be sorry.

Be submissive to everything, open, listening. No fear or shame in the dignity of your experience, language, and knowledge. Be in love with your life.

Great things are not
accomplished by those
who yield to trends and
fads and popular opinion.

An awful realization that
I have been fooling
myself all my life
thinking there was a next
thing to do to keep the
show going and actually
I'm just a sick clown and
so is everybody else...

jack kerouac's
little book of
selected quotes

I believed in a good home, in sane and sound living, in good food, good times, work, faith and hope. I have always believed in these things. It was with some amazement that I realized I was one of the few people in the world who really believed in these things without going around making a dull middle class philosophy out of it. I was suddenly left with nothing in my hands but a handful of crazy stars.

Soon it got dusk, a grapy dusk, a purple dusk over tangerine groves and long melon fields; the sun the color of pressed grapes, slashed with burgandy red, the fields the color of love and Spanish mysteries.

And as far as I can see the
world is too old for us to
talk about it with our
new words.

I felt free and therefore
I was free.

jack kerouac's
little book of
selected quotes

My fault, my failure, is not in the passions I have, but in my lack of control of them.

Happy. Just in my swim
shorts, barefooted, wild-
haired, in the red fire
dark, singing, swigging
wine, spitting, jumping,
running – that's the way
to live. All alone and
free in the soft sands of
the beach.

jack kerouac's
little book of
selected quotes

My witness is the
empty sky.

Nothing behind me,
everything ahead of me,
as is ever so on the road.

jack kerouac's
little book of
selected quotes

Offer them what they
secretly want and they
of course immediately
become panic-stricken.

I want to work in revelations, not just spin silly tales for money. I want to fish as deep down as possible into my own subconscious in the belief that once that far down, everyone will understand because they are the same that far down.

The happiness consists in
realizing that it is all a
great strange dream.

It's okay, girl, we'll make it till the sun goes down forever. And until then what you got to lose but the losing? We're fallen angels who didn't believe that nothing means nothing.

I was having a wonderful
time and the whole world
opened up before me
because I had no dreams.

My life is a vast
inconsequential epic.

jack kerouac's
little book of
selected quotes

I'm right there, swimming
the river of hardships
but I know how to swim.

The closer you get to real
matter, rock air fire and
wood, boy, the more
spiritual the world is.

jack kerouac's
little book of
selected quotes

Don't tell them too much about your soul. They're waiting for just that.

So long and take it easy,
because if you start
taking things seriously,
it is the end of you.

I didn't know what to
say. I felt like crying,
Goddammit everybody
in the world wants an
explanation for your
acts and for your very
being.

Listen closely... the eternal hush of silence goes on and on throughout all this, and has been going on, and will go on and on. This is because the world is nothing but a dream and is just thought of and the everlasting eternity pays no attention to it.

jack kerouac's little book of selected quotes

The beauty of things must
be that they end.

ck kerouac's
ttle book of
ected quotes

There was nothing to talk
about anymore. The only
thing to do was go.

jack kerouac's
little book of
selected quotes

Practice kindness all day
to everybody and you will
realize you're already in
heaven now.

It's all too much and not
enough at the same time.

jack kerouac's
little book of
selected quotes

Life must be rich and full
of loving--it's no good
otherwise, no good at all,
for anyone.

Bop began with Jazz but one afternoon somewhere on a sidewalk maybe 1939, 1940, Dizzy Gillespie or Charlie Parker or Thelonious Monk was walking past a men's clothing store on 42nd Street or South Main in L.A. and from a loudspeaker they suddenly heard a wild impossible mistake in jazz that could only have been heard inside their own imaginary head, and that is a new art. Bop.

jack kerouac's
little book of
selected quotes

While looking for
the light, you may
suddenly be devoured
by the darkness and
find the true light.

Genius gives birth, talent delivers. What Rembrandt or Van Gogh saw in the night can never be seen again. Born writers of the future are amazed already at what they're seeing now, what we'll all see in time for the first time, and then see imitated many times by made writers.

jack kerouac's little book of selected quotes

A pain stabbed my
heart as it did every
time I saw a girl
I loved who was going
the opposite
direction in this
too-big world.

ck kerouac's
ttle book of
ected quotes

Some of my most
neurotically fierce
bitterness is the result
of realizing how untrue
people have become.

jack kerouac's
little book of
selected quotes

Something that you feel
will find its own form.

:k kerouac's
ttle book of
ected quotes

It's good-bye. But we
lean forward to the
next crazy venture
beneath the skies.

Printed in Great Britain
by Amazon